JAMES BALDWIN

A Life from Beginning to End

Copyright © 2021 by Hourly History.

Table of Contents

Introduction

Born in 1924, celebrated author and activist James Baldwin spent his formative years in Harlem—New York City's center of gravity for African Americans at that time. His world was one of both rich culture and deep poverty. Baldwin's teacher Orilla Miller once remarked that James grew up in some of "the worst poverty" she had ever seen.

New York, like much of the rest of the country, would be hit hard when the stock market crashed in 1929; still, Wall Street didn't have much to do with the suffering on Harlem's streets. These problems were systemic and had been baked in long before the onset of the Great Depression. Baldwin would later recall just how destitute life was as a child and how he bore witness to an abundance of violence, drug addicts, and dilapidated housing in the streets of Harlem.

Baldwin's mother, Emma Berdis Jones, was not a native of New York but rather a transplant from Maryland, who had arrived in New York with a wave of Southern migrants looking for more opportunities further north. The identity of Baldwin's biological father remains a mystery, but the man who stepped in to take on the paternal role was David Baldwin, a preacher from whom James would get his last name. David made a living working in factories, where long, grueling shifts barely brought home enough money to get by.

James was just one of nine children in the Baldwin household, and life was hard, but from an early age, he was actively seeking ways to pull himself out of the hardship into which he was born.

Chapter One

Early Life in Harlem

"From Miller, I began to suspect that white people did not act as they did because they were white but for some other reason, and began to try to locate and understand that reason."

—James Baldwin

The man the world would come to know as James Baldwin was born James Arthur Jones on August 2, 1924, in New York City's Harlem Hospital. A few years later, in 1927, his mother married David Baldwin, from whom James would get his now-famous last name. James was always uncomfortable with the fact that he never knew his father, and he expressed this discomfort in his later book, *Nobody Knows My Name*.

The union of James's mother and David Baldwin would produce many children, whom James often ended up babysitting. As James himself once described it, "As they were born, I took them over with one hand and held a book with the other." It sounds almost comical, but from a young age, James learned all about reading, writing, and raising children. Counting George, Barbara, Wilmer, David, Gloria, Ruth, Elizabeth, and Paula, he had eight brothers and sisters in all. Baldwin once humorously described his mother as "given to the exasperating and mysterious habit of having babies."

Being from such a large family during an economic depression would have been hard for anyone, but the prejudice and discrimination so rampant in American life made the situation even worse. David Baldwin faced blatant discrimination on the job, and he often took out his rage on his wife. Privy to all of this, little James did his best to keep himself and his siblings out of the way whenever his stepfather erupted.

It was in an effort to escape some of this volatility at home that James started a habit of spending his free time at local libraries. It was here that he would develop a passion for reading and begin to perfect his craft. As Baldwin would later put it, "I read my way through two libraries by the time I was thirteen. I read myself out of Harlem."

As much as he was prone to go on a tirade, James's father did have a softer side, and one of his healthier outlets was his work with local Pentecostal churches. Baldwin would later describe his father as a "Pentecostal storefront preacher." The family initially went to Harlem's famed Abyssinian Baptist Church before switching to the Mount Calvary of the Pentecostal Faith Church, which was known by the locals as simply Mother Horn's Church since it was pastored by Rosa Horn.

James Baldwin himself would initially be an enthusiastic churchgoer, enthralled by "the excitement and ecstasy of worship, music, poetry, and communion." Biblical sermons also had a significant influence on how James would approach his own writing. He had a unique way with words from a young age, and his school teachers quickly took note. One of them, a certain Orilla Miller, was so impressed by a play that Baldwin had crafted that she sought to take little James under her wing.

According to Miller's later recollection, she knew there was something special about Baldwin from the very beginning. She would later recall, "I realized that he was just a remarkable child." Miller herself came from an interesting background. She originally hailed from the Midwest, but upon graduating from Antioch

College, she came to New York. Here, she became both politically and culturally active, making a point to join the CPU (Communist Party of the United States), as well as getting a job with the FTP (Federal Theatre Project). In 1935, Miller was assigned to teach young children at a public school in Harlem; this is where she and James crossed paths.

As their relationship grew, Miller wished to nurture the child's creativity by taking him to see theatrical productions in New York City. This may sound like a nice gesture, but this teacher's efforts would set off a firestorm at Baldwin's home due to his stepfather's own internal prejudice. Miller was a white woman, and David Baldwin—who had suffered through racism his whole life—had developed what James Baldwin later described as an outright hatred of white people. According to Baldwin biographer James Campbell, "David Baldwin hated white people, and his devotion to God was mixed with a hope that God would take revenge on them for him." In the end, however, David Baldwin was overruled by James's mother, and he was allowed to go to the theater with Miller regardless.

Orilla Miller and James shared many literary interests, but in particular, they were both very fond of the British author Charles Dickens. The two would have long conversations about the characters that were presented in Dickens' masterpiece *A Tale of Two Cities*. In 1936, Miller would take James to see a film adaptation of the novel. It was wonderful for him to see the narrative he had read so often come to life like this. After this outing, Miller took James to watch a theatrical production of *Macbeth* produced by Orson Welles. In this version of the play, the backdrop for the story had been changed to the island of Haiti, and all of the actors Orson used were African Americans.

Along with this exposure to the arts, Orilla Miller and her husband Evan exposed James Baldwin to political intrigue, for it was right around this time that Evan took James to a May Day parade hosted by local communist organizers. Here, Baldwin saw people of all backgrounds actively seeking change. He did not always agree with the principles presented, but this idea of revolutionary solidarity would stick with him for the rest of his life.

Chapter Two

The Young Preacher

"Confronted with the impossibility of remaining faithful to one's beliefs, and the equal impossibility of becoming free of them, one can be driven to the most inhuman excesses."

—James Baldwin

In 1936, James Baldwin was 12 years old and had just begun attending Harlem's Frederick Douglass Junior High School. Here, he would meet another early mentor in the form of a math teacher named Herman W. Porter. Porter would later recall Baldwin's literary ability as being "better than anyone in the school—from the principal on down."

As well as being a math instructor, Porter was the faculty advisor for the school's magazine, a periodical called *The Douglass Pilot*. Taking note of Baldwin's abilities, Porter recruited him to write for the magazine. Just like Orilla Miller before him, Porter was so impressed with the young man's abilities that he was determined to intervene in his life.

It was during one of these interventions that Porter came to the Baldwin residence to take the teenager with him to the public library to research some material for future articles for the magazine. Upon his arrival at the Baldwin abode, he was amazed at what he saw. He described the living conditions as being "unbelievably poverty-stricken."

According to Porter, Baldwin's mother answered the door with a whole "gaggle of youngsters" immediately underfoot. After meeting her and all of James's brothers and sisters, Porter was then introduced to David Baldwin, who grudgingly gave his permission for Porter to escort young James down to the library. The two took the bus to get there. During the course of the bus ride, Porter became concerned for his student, noticing that he seemed a little anxious. James was indeed feeling a bit high-strung due to the pressures he faced in life, and he demonstrated as much by throwing up as soon as the pair disembarked. Fortunately, James was able to get a hold of himself in the end, and he and Porter went to the library as planned.

Once there, they hit the books. It was from this impromptu session that James would produce his first piece for the school magazine entitled, "Harlem—Then and Now." It was an academic and reflective piece in which he considered the history of Harlem from the bygone past to the present. In the article, James asked, "I wonder how many of us have ever stopped to think what Harlem was like two or three centuries ago? Or how it came to be as it is today?" James then answers that question by remarking, "Not many of us. Most of us know in a vague way that the Dutch lived in Harlem 'a long time ago,' and let it go at that. We don't think about how the Indians were driven out, how the Dutch and English fought, or how finally Harlem grew into what it is today."

In those days, young Baldwin felt a flux of forces pulling on him in different directions. With the encouragement of his mentors at school, he suspected that the best course in life for him was to become a writer. At the same time, however, he had become more involved with the local church. One church, in particular, the Fireside Pentecostal Assembly, had become his favorite place of worship.

Some might think that Baldwin's delving into intellectual works, and even communist ideas, might not have been compatible with the church, but during this period of adjustment, James Baldwin was still very much interested in religion. At the Fireside Pentecostal Assembly, the now 14-year-old James would often get up on stage and give sermons. He enjoyed the feeling of preaching and the interaction with the audience so much that he told his mother at the time, "There's nothing I want to do more than preach." Since his parents were both deeply religious, this was certainly welcome news.

James Baldwin grew up in the church, and he knew the Bible front and back. In fact, the good book was probably the first book he had ever read. Baldwin was gifted at not only memorizing scripture but at paraphrasing them and inserting Bible verses into a perfect stitchwork of a larger message. Even as his peers were beginning to experiment with drugs, alcohol, and sex, at this stage in his development, James steadfastly abstained from it all, feeling that he had a higher calling to fulfill.

Chapter Three

From Harlem to the Bronx

"I knew I was black, of course, but I also knew I was smart. I didn't know how I would use my mind, or even if I could, but that was the only thing I had to use."

—James Baldwin

After finishing his studies at Frederick Douglass Junior High School, James Baldwin moved on to DeWitt Clinton High. Located in the Bronx, DeWitt Clinton High would have James hopping onto a train every day to get to class on time. Being able to leave Harlem and see the world outside of his usual stomping grounds was an eye-opening experience for him.

The Bronx was full of immigrants at that time and a real melting pot of culture. Baldwin would make a lot of friends at his new school, one of them being a future author himself, Emile

Capouya. James and Emile would work together on the high school's magazine called *TheMagpie*. Baldwin excelled in these endeavors as he ensured that his high school publication achieved a state of excellence. It was in *TheMagpie* that he would also contribute some unique and stirring poetry. One of the most memorable poems, called "Black Girl Shouting," addressed the terrible tragedy of lynchings that were occurring in the South:

"Black girl, stretch
Your mouth so wide.
None will guess
The way he died
Turned your heart
To quivering mud
While your lover's
Soft, red blood
Stained the scowling
Outraged tree.
Angels come
To cut him free!"

This poem perfectly captured the somber outrage over the senseless violence that was occurring in certain parts of America at the time. Most who read this poem are impressed by its context, sense of timing, and raw emotion—so much so that many have often wondered why Baldwin didn't write more pieces like this. Later in life, Baldwin would reveal that he became discouraged with his poetry when a well-meaning mentor—the poet and novelist Countee Cullen—told him that his work was "an awful lot like Hughes." Cullen was, of course, referring to the great African American poet Langston Hughes. He wasn't really trying to say that Baldwin was copying Hughes, just that his work sounded similar to it. Yet, the remark seemed to bother James and made him change course.

It was around this time that James began to take a different direction in his religious life as well. His days of being a firebrand preacher were far behind him by the time he turned 17. From this point forward, Baldwin would identify himself as being non-religious. Nevertheless, he would have a complicated relationship with religion for the rest of his life. On some occasions, he would praise religion as liberating, yet at other times, he would claim that religion was oppressive.

It was also around this time that Baldwin began to open up sexually and accept the fact that he was attracted to other men. A chance encounter with a man named Beauford Delaney would prove pivotal in this acceptance. Delaney was a local artist—a painter—based out of Greenwich Village. Baldwin was made aware of Delaney through his friend Emile Capouya, and the impression he made on the young man was enormous. Delaney was an African American artist from a religious background just like Baldwin, and he was also openly gay. These facts were not lost on James at all; here was a man who looked similar to him, who was both living out his dream of being an artist, as well as being fully accepting of his own sexual identity.

Delaney, a big jazz fan, also introduced Baldwin to a new world of culture and music. As soon as Baldwin stepped into his home, he was greeted by this vibrancy. As Baldwin described it, "I walked into music. I had grown up with music, but now, on Beauford's small black record player, I began to hear what I had never dared or been able to hear."

At this point, Baldwin decided to break with his old church-going life and instead throw himself headlong into a bohemian culture that he felt was both rewarding and refreshing. He had found a world of his own, and he was determined never to leave it.

Chapter Four

Baldwin During World War II

"I imagine one of the reasons people cling to their hates so stubbornly is because they sense, once hate is gone, they will be forced to deal with pain."

—James Baldwin

Baldwin graduated from DeWitt Clinton High in 1942. Upon graduating, James had planned to attend a public university in New York City called City College, but he didn't have enough money for school. His family needed his support more than ever, so he decided to get a job instead. World War II had just recently reached American shores with the attack on Pearl Harbor, and so for a change, jobs were quite plentiful since the U.S. government had all kinds of openings in manufacturing and other jobs vital to the war effort.

Baldwin ended up getting a job with his high school friend Emile Capouya at an army depot in Princeton, New Jersey. For this job, he laid down new track for the depot's railroad. Baldwin opted to live on-site, paying for his room and board in Jersey while regularly sending money to his family back in New York. Although it was great for him to be able to live on his own and not only support himself but also support his other family members, the job had a definite downside. It was hard labor, and Baldwin was periodically subjected to discrimination.

Of his time working in Jersey, Baldwin would later reflect, "I learned in New Jersey that to be a Negro meant, precisely, that one was never looked at but was simply at the mercy of the reflexes one's skin caused in other people." Forced to work in such a hostile environment, Baldwin soon couldn't help but feel that there was a conspiracy at work against him. He would later say, "It began to seem that the machinery of the organization I worked for was turning over, day and night, with but one aim: to eject me." Baldwin was in fact fired from the job shortly thereafter.

It was in Jersey, trying to strike it out on his own for the first time, that James first felt discrimination in a very personal way. As he bounced around from one job to another, the daily discrimination was starting to get to him. Baldwin resented it, and he wanted to fight against it somehow. On one particular night, he went to an upscale restaurant he absolutely knew would display prejudice toward him so that he could lash out. As Baldwin put it, "I knew not even the intercession of the Virgin would cause me to be served."

Yet, he demanded service regardless. When the waitress bluntly informed him in the vernacular of the day, "We don't serve Negroes here," the rage and disgust inside James Baldwin finally reached a breaking point, and he was ready to explode. Baldwin later recalled, "There was nothing on the table but an ordinary water mug full of water, and I picked this up and hurled it with all my strength at her. She ducked and it missed her and shattered against the mirror behind the bar."

Baldwin then described how he fled the scene as a group of angry patrons tried to chase after him. He managed to get away, but he realized that he had very nearly crossed a point of no return. As Baldwin would put it, "My life, my real life, was in danger, and not from anything other people might do but from the hatred I carried in my own heart."

Baldwin realized that the discrimination he suffered on a daily basis was filling him with rage, and if he wasn't careful, he might do something he would regret later on. He recalled being so angry he could have killed someone. If while in the throes of rage, he had done something drastic that night, his life as he knew it would be over. Quite simply, it would be the end of his dreams of being a writer if he were sent to prison. Baldwin knew the cards were stacked against him, but if he wanted to escape the unjust system he was trapped in, he would have to control himself and bide his time just a little while longer.

Chapter Five

The Harlem Riots

"You think your pain and your heartbreak are unprecedented in the history of the world, but then you read."

—James Baldwin

After leaving Jersey for good, Baldwin moved back in with his parents in Harlem, and for a short time, he got a job at a meatpacking plant. However, he faced a lot of the same problems here, too, and parted ways with it shortly thereafter. In between jobs, Baldwin began to put some time in at a local writers' workshop held at the Writers' School of the League of American Writers. This was a group of dedicated writers and literary critics sponsored by the U.S. Communist Party.

During World War II, the United States was not yet shutting down organizations with communist ties. The start of the Cold War and McCarthyism was still a few years away, and communist groups were, for the most part, able to conduct business out in the open. The communists were particularly busy in New York, aligning themselves with left-wing causes and activists whenever they could. When it came to the problem of discrimination, the communists sought to insert themselves into the mix as well. The communist-supported League is said to have been actively seeking to recruit black members and support black culture as a means to generate interest among the African American community. Here, Baldwin worked on a team along with 20 other writers, and he was eventually awarded a scholarship for his efforts.

Not too long after this, James received the news that his stepfather—the only father figure he had known—had passed. His father's health had been deteriorating for some time, and so when he died on July 29, 1943, it wasn't exactly unexpected, but nevertheless, the timing of it was nothing short of bizarre. It was on the very day of David Baldwin's death that his youngest child—and James's youngest sibling—was born. The day of his funeral also just so happened to be James's 19th birthday. Yet even more memorable for James, considering the seething anger his father held due to the discriminatory conditions of society, Harlem erupted in riots on the same day as the funeral.

Harlem was already a tinder box of tension, and this was neither the first nor the last riot to take place in the area. The incident that ignited the inferno this time was customary enough. A woman at a local hotel had apparently become upset and was causing a scene, but when police tried to arrest her for disorderly conduct, an African American soldier intervened. The police didn't take too kindly to this interference, so they attempted to arrest the soldier on charges of disorderly conduct as well.

During the scuffle, the police opened fire, and the African American soldier was struck in the shoulder by a bullet. It was just a flesh wound, but somehow or other, a rumor was spread that the soldier had been killed by police. The African American community, already frustrated with discrimination at home, were naturally outraged at the idea that one of their own brave young men, who had fought overseas for the United States, would come home only to get shot and killed by the police. Again, the soldier was not killed, but people had heard that he was, and a riot erupted in Harlem as a result.

All of this happened just a matter of days after Baldwin's stepfather made his exit from this world. James, at 19 years old, was now the man of the family and in desperate need of work. Still, he wasn't ready to go back to manual labor; he sought instead to get into the business of literature any way he could. At one point, Baldwin worked as a messenger for a progressive paper called *PM*. Then, in the fall of 1944, he got a job as a galley boy for the *Morning Telegraph*.

It was during this period that Baldwin carried on a correspondence with a friend of his, Tom Martin. Martin had worked with Baldwin laying track before being sent off to Italy to fight in the war. In these letters, Tom reveals his deep affection for Baldwin, by calling James the "dark love of my life." Back in those days, affection between two men was kept quiet, but the undercurrents here are pretty clear.

In the meantime, James was living the life of a closeted gay man, experimenting with different lovers, while trying desperately to keep that fact secret from his religious family. It was the elements of this struggle of both finding himself and shielding himself at the same time that would become recurring themes in many of Baldwin's future works.

At any rate, James felt like the walls were closing in on him, and he needed an escape. Taking a cue from his old friend Beauford Delaney, he decided to move to Greenwich Village. He felt bad about no longer supporting his family, but he knew that he had to find a way to support himself before he could help anyone else. As Baldwin would later put it, "I had to jump then, or I would quite simply have died." And so, James Baldwin finally made a break for it. He said goodbye to the desolate trappings of his childhood home and left Harlem fully determined to never look back.

Chapter Six

Early Literary Work

"It is true that the more one learns, the less one knows."

—James Baldwin

Upon moving to Greenwich Village, Baldwin stayed with his friend Delaney before eking it out on his own in various rentals. Initially, he worked a series of part-time jobs just to get by, but one day, Delaney introduced him to a woman from Trinidad named Connie Williams. Williams was the owner of a local diner called the Calypso. She approached Baldwin, asking him if he would like to be a waiter. Considering the dismal job prospects and the fact that the Calypso would at least provide a friendly, bohemian environment for the budding writer, James agreed.

It might not have been the most glamorous of jobs, but it was certainly better than doing hard physical labor like he had done at the railroad and the other grueling jobs that he had worked.

Connie was also very loving, kind, and supportive. In many ways, Baldwin began to view her as a surrogate mother, and he greatly benefited from the warmth she projected. If he found himself suddenly without a roof over his head, Williams was always willing to let him crash for the night at her place.

The Calypso quickly became a frequent hangout for Baldwin and his Greenwich friends. According to Baldwin, he and his entourage "held court" at the place after everyone else had left. It wasn't just James and his friends that hung out at the Calypso—soon, a whole cadre of intellectuals, activists, and even budding celebrities were regular faces at the establishment. Among them were Marlon Brando, Burt Lancaster, Eartha Kitt, Paul Robeson, Alain Locke, Claude McKay, and occasionally even Malcolm X made an appearance.

The conversation was always lively, and Baldwin himself became known for his eloquent speaking ability. Just like he had enthralled parishioners at the Fireside Pentecostal Assembly in years prior, he now had a new captive audience at the Calypso.

Baldwin was still forming his identity by this time, and as it pertained to his sexual identity, he was seeing both men and women, even though he confided in his old friend Emile Capouya that he considered himself to be gay. Nevertheless, after getting involved with a woman named Grace, Baldwin claims he fell in love, and for a time, he even considered getting married. In the end, however, he decided that it just wouldn't work. Baldwin would later recall thinking that although it was possible for him to love women, he was always better off when he refrained from "making love to them."

During this period, Baldwin also became very close to a man named Eugene Worth. Worth was a member of the Young People's Socialist League, and the two would spend much time together discussing their thoughts on political ideology and social issues such as poverty and racial discrimination. Worth would meet a tragic end, however, as he committed suicide by jumping off of the George Washington Bridge in 1946. Baldwin would later model one of his characters in his book *Another Country* after this man's tragic life.

Another key figure that Baldwin met during this period was the actor and Calypso regular Marlon Brando. Brando was a social activist early on, and he and Baldwin bonded over their beliefs.

By the time Brando was making a name for himself by performing in the theatrical production of Tennessee Williams' *A Streetcar Named Desire* in 1947, the two had cemented a friendship that would last a lifetime.

Baldwin's literary career, meanwhile, was facing many twists and turns as he tried to navigate his way through the world of publishing. In the early 1940s, Baldwin had been working on an autobiographical work he called *Crying Holy*. He was seeking a publisher to support his efforts but didn't know where to start. Then, in 1944, he made the acquaintance of Richard Wright, who was already a celebrated writer for his 1940 work *Native Son*.

Baldwin shared his unfinished manuscript with Wright, and Wright then passed it along to Harper and Brothers—the same publishing company that had produced Wright's own books. The outlook of Harper and Brothers toward Baldwin was initially quite positive, and they offered him a $500 grant to keep pushing forward with *Crying Holy*. Not long thereafter though, they ended up rejecting the book altogether.

Ultimately, Baldwin's first publication wouldn't come until 1947 when his book review of Maxim Gorky's *Best Short Stories* appeared in the progressive magazine *The Nation*. It was a good first step, but Baldwin had other problems to contend with, for it was around this time that the Cold War between the capitalist United States and the communist Soviet Union was starting.

Even though Soviet Russia had been an ally during World War II, after the war, the Iron Curtain had descended upon Europe, separating the Eastern Soviet bloc from the Western democracies. Suddenly, in America, anyone with leftist ties to socialist or communist groups was viewed with suspicion. Baldwin, already feeling like an outsider due to his race and sexuality, was now doubly isolated due to his political leanings. As the McCarthy hearings began to take place, which actively hunted down anyone suspected to have communist sympathies, Baldwin became increasingly disillusioned with the prospect of life in the United States.

It was for all of these reasons and more that, in November of 1948, Baldwin ran off to Paris, France. It was certainly a drastic step on his part, especially considering the fragile state of his finances (he had just $40 to survive on), but Baldwin felt like he just had to get away.

Chapter Seven

Exile in Paris

"Perhaps the turning point in one's life is realizing that to be treated like a victim is not necessarily to become one."

—James Baldwin

Paris, France, was in the late 1940s still recovering from the ravages of World War II. Yet even amidst the rubble, artistically minded individuals from all over the globe still flocked to this great city, hoping to find the intellectual freedom they so desperately craved. James Baldwin was one of them.

Baldwin initially enjoyed the French atmosphere, feeling that he was finally free from the socially ingrained prejudices of America, but it didn't take him long to realize that France had its own set of discriminatory standards. For the French, someone like James Baldwin—an American from the West—was a rare, almost exotic find. Without the same history of oppression, James didn't feel the same kind of discomfort he often felt in America. Yet, as James became acquainted with France's own local minority populations, he found that they were being discriminated against by the French in similar ways that European Americans discriminated against African Americans back home in the United States.

Particularly distressing to him was the French treatment of Algerians. Algeria, a country located in North Africa, had been a French colony for some time, and after the war, a significantly weakened France was trying desperately to hold onto this foothold on the African continent. Baldwin found an immediate affinity with these Algerian migrants in France and made many friends among their diaspora. He felt a natural affinity with them as he recognized in their plight, his own.

During this time, he also reconnected with African American writer Richard Wright. Wright had made the move to France about a year before Baldwin. Like Baldwin, he was afraid that his political activism would come under scrutiny during the heightening of the Cold War, and so, he had decided to set up shop in Paris instead. Along with Wright, Baldwin also became acquainted with the American novelist Truman Capote.

Considering the experiences of expats like himself and his colleagues, Baldwin began to work on a novel during this time in which detailed what he felt it was like to be an American in general—and an African American in particular—exiled abroad.

In the end though, what would send shockwaves across the Atlantic was an essay Baldwin crafted in the spring of 1949 for a publication of *Zero* magazine. Here, Baldwin critiqued the genre of the so-called "protest novel." These were fictional narratives written by well-meaning if not often misguided activists to make a point about various social causes. First, Baldwin criticized the most iconic protest novel of all—Harriet Beecher Stowe's *Uncle Tom's Cabin*. This book, written in 1852, condemned slavery and was considered pivotal in changing the hearts and minds of Americans over the practice. In later years, however, its depiction of African Americans has been highly criticized. This was something that Baldwin himself took issue with.

He lambasted Beecher's work as being nothing more than a "bad novel" with "self-righteous, virtuous sentimentality" that actually covered up "a mask of cruelty." He compared this to the sentimental protest novels of his day, in which left-leaning liberals supposedly protested injustices while at the same time making complete caricatures of their subjects. But where Baldwin set off a firestorm within his own social circle was when he lumped his friend Richard Wright into the bunch, claiming that his book *Native Son* was a continuation of this trope.

In the book *Native Son*, Wright's character, an African American called Bigger Thomas, gets into trouble when he accidentally kills a white woman. Although Baldwin had previously praised Wright's storytelling, in this critique, he seemed to find the stereotypes present in the book unbearable. Baldwin expressed, "Below the surface of this novel there lies, as it seems to me, a continuation, a complement of that monstrous legend it was written to destroy." These words were pretty searing, but Baldwin had more. Bringing it all together, he concluded, "The failure of the protest novel lies in its rejection of life, the human being, the denial of his beauty, dread, power, in its insistence that it is his categorization alone with is real and which cannot be transcended."

There was immediate outrage from many corners of the literary world when Baldwin penned this piece. They thought it was awful presumptuous of a 25-year-old unpublished novelist to attack a seasoned and celebrated writer like Richard Wright. Baldwin would later regret some of his words, even while sticking by them. In regard to the venomous tone he took toward his friend, he would later analyze himself and remark, "Unconsciously I think I turned [Richard Wright] into my father, not the father that I knew."

It was as if James Baldwin was excoriating his old mentor and artistic father figure as a means of charting his own course through the emotional wilderness he had found himself trapped in.

Chapter Eight

Baldwin's First Novel

"No one can possibly know what is about to happen: it is happening, each time, for the first time, for the only time."

—James Baldwin

On the heels of shaking up the literary world with his essay called "Everybody's Protest Novel," James Baldwin was finishing up what would become his own first published novel, an autobiographically driven narrative called *Go Tell It on the Mountain*. Before he managed to do that though, he had some immediate financial difficulties to get over.

Baldwin was at this point just about broke and spent the summer clerking for an American lawyer to bring in an income. His health was also failing him during this period, and he was in and out of the hospital due to an inflamed gland. In addition to these problems, he had managed to run afoul of the police in December of 1949 as he was arrested on charges of being a receiver of stolen goods. This arrest had to do with a missing bed sheet from a hotel. Baldwin had borrowed the bedsheet in question from a friend of his, and it was the friend who had stolen the sheet from a hotel. When this bedsheet was tracked down to Baldwin, he and his friend were arrested for its theft.

Upon being taken to a jail cell, Baldwin was struck with how routine it was for Algerian minorities in France to be arrested and locked up. Considering these North Africans behind French prison bars, Baldwin would later write that "the truth was that they were far more realistic about the world than I, and more nearly right about it." These thoughts and feelings would later find their way into Baldwin's essay "Equal in Paris."

Upon getting out of jail, Baldwin was as strapped for cash as ever—so much so that he asked for one of his editors to loan him money. Meanwhile, he continued to work on what would become the final draft of *Go Tell It on the Mountain*. Also around this time, James began a serious relationship with a Swiss artist by the name of Lucien Happersberger. Baldwin had met Happersberger in Paris soon after he first arrived in France, and by 1950, they were intimately involved with each other. Lucien was a man of torn affections, however, and to James's sadness, he ended up breaking off their relationship to marry a Swiss woman by the name of Suzie.

Nevertheless, the two would remain friends, and Baldwin would even be made a godfather of Lucien and Suzie's children. Shortly after their marriage, Baldwin even lived with the couple, staying at their family cottage in Switzerland over the winter months of 1951. It was here that Baldwin would craft the essay "Stranger in the Village," which would appear in a 1953 issue of *Harper's Magazine* before being published in his collection of essays, *Notes of a Native Son*, in 1955.

In this piece, Baldwin speaks of his alienation, not just of being a stranger in a strange land but of feeling alienated from history. Thinking of the Swiss people wrapped up in their personal traditions and considering his own ancestry as an African American, Baldwin observed, "Out of their hymns and dances comes Beethoven and Bach. Go back a few centuries and they are in their full glory—but I am in Africa, watching the conquerors arrive."

It was while Baldwin was holed up in Switzerland that he finally finished up his autobiographical narrative *Go Tell It on the Mountain*. It took him nearly ten years to complete this masterpiece, but he was glad that he persevered. He aimed for this work to highlight social dysfunction but manage to go beyond the "protest novel" format that he had so roundly criticized in the past.

One of the main themes of the narrative would be how African American families originating from the South looked toward the North as a kind of promised land. Baldwin shares through personal experience that the promised land of the North was not all it was cracked up to be. The book also focused on Baldwin's repressed feelings of homosexual attraction while growing up in the church. This is embodied in the form of two of the main characters John and Elisha who end up realizing their passion for each other.

The book was picked up by the publishing house Knopf in May of 1953, and once published, it received good reviews. Even the great poet Langston Hughes praised the book but also offended Baldwin's sensibilities by referring to it as a "low-down story in a velvet bag." In other words, Hughes was insinuating that the tale was tawdry yet dressed up to look like something nice. Baldwin wouldn't forget this slight, and the two would enter into a prolonged grudge match, in a similar fashion as he had entered into with the esteemed novelist Richard Wright. Like always, Baldwin was a man who held fast to his convictions no matter what.

Chapter Nine

Depression and Suicide Attempt

"This was perhaps the first time in my life that death occurred to me as a reality. I thought of the people before me who had looked down at the river and gone to sleep beneath it."

—James Baldwin

By the mid-1950s, the writing career of James Baldwin seemed promising. His masterwork, *Go Tell It on the Mountain*, was doing well, and he was just beginning to become financially secure. His personal relationships, however, still left a lot to be desired when it came to stability.

One of his rockier relationships was with a man named Arnold. Baldwin adored Arnold, although they regularly fought. It was right after one of these tumultuous occasions in 1956 that Baldwin finally reached a breaking point and attempted to take his own life. He called a good friend of his—Mary Painter—who worked at the U.S. embassy in France and gave her some alarming news; he informed her that he had just taken an inordinate amount of sleeping pills and was waiting for the end to come. Mary, frightened that her friend might perish, ran right over to Baldwin's side, where she forced him to vomit and give up the attempt. Still, this would not be his last attempt.

Baldwin struggled with bouts of depression and nervous breakdowns throughout his life, and suicide was a frequent theme in his writing. In the prior year, he had followed up *Go Tell It on the Mountain* with a compilation of essays and reviews, which he published under the title *Notes of a Native Son*. The name was an obvious nod to his one-time mentor, current antagonist, Richard Wright's *Native Son*. In the preface of the book, Baldwin left a pointed disclaimer that summed up his sentiments and disposition at the time. He proclaimed, "I love America more than any other country in the world, and exactly for this reason, I insist on the right to criticize her perpetually."

Baldwin got right to the point with these words. Even though he was often highly critical of America, for him, it was still a decent place. Many may find Baldwin's sentiments hard to believe, but his experience overseas had opened his eyes to realize that much of the oppression and dysfunction he had grown up thinking was a product of America was much more a universal flaw of humankind. He had witnessed the French mistreating North Africans just as badly as the NYPD treated him back in the States.

Close on the heels of *Notes of a Native Son*, Baldwin switched gears yet again and began work on writing a play, which he called *The Amen Corner*. This piece drew heavily on his own experience growing up in Harlem in the church and has a female pastor as the main character, Margaret Alexander, who isn't unlike the Pentecostal Mother Horn of his youth.

In the play, Margaret has to grapple with societal conflict and how best to deal with the social pressures that her son David and her husband Luke are experiencing. As Baldwin described it, she was trying to figure out "how to treat her husband and her son as men and at the same time to protect them from bloody consequences of trying to be a man in this society." To Baldwin's delight, the play took off, and the production was made. As a boy, he had enjoyed the theater for the first time due to the kindness of his teacher, Orilla Miller; now, he was writing plays of his own.

Baldwin had indeed come a long way, and if all this wasn't enough, another hidden gem Baldwin had waiting in the wings, a novel called *Giovanni's Room*, was picked up by Dial Press. Set in Paris, France, this book would also take aspects from Baldwin's life but through entirely fictional characters. This book, featuring intrigue, love triangles, and introspection, received rave reviews.

Baldwin was relishing all of these accolades abroad when developments back in the States began to capture his attention. In 1957, American civil rights activists were rallying to pass legislation to improve the lives of African Americans. In particular, activists were mobilizing to ensure that the 1957 Civil Rights Act would be passed in Congress. Among other things, a primary focus of the 1957 Civil Rights Act was the integration of schools. President Eisenhower, a Republican, was favorable to the Act, but a coalition of hostile Southern Democrats were against it.

For modern readers who may not be familiar with the dynamics of the day, even though Democrats were later associated with the civil rights movement, back in the 1950s, many Democrats were against it. This began to dramatically change when John F. Kennedy took office in 1960. In the 1950s, however, it was still the Republicans who were considered the primary champions for the civil rights movement. It was also under Eisenhower that the Supreme Court ruled that school segregation was "inherently unequal," leading the Eisenhower administration to enforce the ruling when Southern Democrats tried to block school integration.

At any rate, it was after he had heard of all of these efforts underway to improve the lives of African Americans that James Baldwin was inspired to head to the United States himself to see what he could do to help. In the summer of 1957, Baldwin hopped on a boat and traveled across the Atlantic back home to New York. The homecoming was a difficult one, or as Baldwin described it in a letter to Mary Painter, "I am in another country, briefly, but this country is in the difficult world: things are not going well here."

Shortly after his arrival in the U.S., Baldwin began talks with *Partisan Review* to go on assignment as a reporter on the civil rights movement in the South. On September 9, meanwhile, Eisenhower had officially signed the

Civil Rights Act of 1957 into law, meaning that Southern schools would have to comply with integration. Shortly thereafter, Baldwin was sent off to Charlotte, North Carolina, where the local governance was attempting to defy these calls for integration. Once on the ground, he interviewed students who were trying to attend previously segregated schools.

From Charlotte, Baldwin then went to the even more famous flashpoint of the civil rights movement—Little Rock, Arkansas. Here, he joined up with Daisy Bates, an activist for the NAACP (National Association for the Advancement of Coloured People). Bates was also a publisher for *The Arkansas State Press*, which covered the case of the "Little Rock Nine." The Little Rock Nine was a group of African American youths who enrolled at Little Rock's previously segregated Central High School. They faced both verbal and physical abuse as they attempted to take their place in this previously all-white school and, in the end, had to be protected by federal troops to even get in the front door.

After finishing up his reporting in Little Rock, Baldwin then headed over to Atlanta, Georgia, where he met with civil rights activist and leader Martin Luther King, Jr. Baldwin was deeply impressed by King, and in a letter to Mary Painter shortly thereafter, he called him a "great man." After meeting with King, Baldwin went to Birmingham, Alabama, where he had an audience with a close aid of King's—Reverend Fred Shuttlesworth. Shuttlesworth was one of the founders of the Southern Christian Leadership Conference, an early church-based champion of the civil rights movement. From Birmingham, Baldwin then went to Montgomery, where he met with King's wife, Coretta Scott King.

Baldwin learned much during his travels across America's South, but it was emotionally exhausting. After completing his assignment, he returned to France, where he would remark, "I don't think I have ever suffered before as I have these last few months."

Chapter Ten

Baldwin and the Civil Rights Movement

"Not everything that is faced can be changed, but nothing can be changed until it is faced."

—James Baldwin

By the time 1958 rolled around, James Baldwin had left the United States and was back in Paris. Since France was right in the middle of its war with Algeria at that time, he had seemingly left one hotbed of social unrest for another. His observations of these troubles appeared in an essay called "Paris, '58," which summed up his thoughts and feelings on the matter. Here, he once again drew parallels between how Algerians were treated by the French and how African Americans were being treated by European Americans in the United States. Baldwin argued that "American Negroes had not been hated as long as they were slaves; they began to be hated when they were slaves no longer. And the French did not hate Algerians ten years ago. They scarcely knew that Algerians existed. But they are beginning to hate them now."

Baldwin then further observed how the European powers were so quick to subdue and colonize big chunks of the planet but then found themselves getting uneasy when the very people they colonized decided to relocate to their own European capitals. Baldwin mused, "It was all very well to have dark Frenchmen and Englishmen in the colonies; but it was never expected that these people would actually use their passports, certainly never in such numbers, to cause trouble on the mainland, change the structure of the government, and endanger the peace of the capital."

When he wasn't writing about political happenings, Baldwin turned once again to semi-autobiographical narratives. This would eventually result in a book called *Another Country*. The main character of the novel, Rufus, was based on Baldwin's old friend from New York, Eugene Worth, who had taken his own life. His work on this book would take up much of his time in 1959.

In a letter to Mary Painter during this period, Baldwin complained, "Writing a novel is just . . . hard work, from the time you begin the damn thing until it finally falls from your arthritic fingers." A perfectionist, Baldwin wasn't one to quickly hammer out books. For him, it was painstaking work with revision after revision, and the completed draft of *Another Country* would not be available to the world until 1962.

The civil rights movement in the United States would capture Baldwin's attention once again in the meantime when he heard reports of African Americans boldly defying segregated establishments by holding "sit-ins." Back in those days, a sit-in was when African Americans sat down in segregated facilities, demanding to receive service. Such things struck a personal chord with Baldwin since he had experienced being turned away from restaurants and diners himself during his youth.

Ready to report on these happenings, Baldwin headed back to the United States and ended up in Florida in May of 1960, where he began reporting for *Mademoiselle* magazine. From his perch in Florida, Baldwin fired off a letter to Martin Luther King, Jr, who was in Atlanta at the time. This led to Baldwin heading to meet King for a personal interview. Not long after conducting this fateful interview with King, Baldwin soon found himself back in his old stomping grounds of New York, where he gave a speech at a strike rally in January of 1961.

By this point, Baldwin was starting to receive some unwanted attention from the FBI. Always looking for radicals in those days, Baldwin's increasing relevance to social justice movements put him on the FBI's radar, and they would continue to monitor him for several years to come. All of these experiences would end up becoming a part of Baldwin's book *The Fire Next Time*, which was published in 1963.

After this latest stint in America came to a close, Baldwin began a mini sight-seeing tour overseas that led him first to Israel and then to Istanbul, Turkey. It was in Istanbul in late 1961 that he finally completed his final draft of *Another Country*. The book sold exceedingly well but had some mixed reviews, primarily due to its sexual content. The sensibilities of some were so offended, in fact, that the book was even flagged for possible obscenity by the FBI.

Nevertheless, it was an exciting time for Baldwin, and he relished the success. He was in a celebratory mood, and in the summer of 1962, he decided to go on an excursion with his sister Gloria to the African continent. Baldwin had never been to Africa before and ended up making a grand tour that took him to Ghana, Senegal, and Sierra Leone.

By 1963, he was back in America, where he was once again drawn to events relating to the civil rights movement. He went on several speaking engagements in which he voiced his views on race relations in America. *Time* magazine took note of Baldwin's speeches and was inspired enough to put him on the cover of their magazine in May of 1963, with an article that praised the way Baldwin voiced "with such poignancy and abrasiveness the dark realities of the racial ferment in North and South."

Yet the highlight of Baldwin's latest tour of the United States by far was his participation in the 1963 March on Washington where Martin Luther King, Jr. gave his legendary "I Have a Dream" speech. Baldwin continued his activism throughout much of the 1960s, participating in marches in the South and using his voice as a celebrity for causes when he thought it was possible that he could make a difference.

One of these causes involved defending a group of Harlem youths accused of murder.

Known as the "Harlem Six," this group of young men were accused of killing Frank and Margit Sugar at their shop in Harlem. There were problems with the case from the beginning since it came to be known that the police had specifically targeted some of the suspects because of their previous participation in protests. The case created quite a bit of tension in the area, as the Harlem Six ended up being found guilty of murder and handed out life sentences.

Baldwin used his star power to raise money for a new trial for the young men. Ultimately, the convictions would be overturned in 1968 since it was determined that their confessions had been extracted under severe coercion—in other words, through police beatings. While Baldwin waded through these developments, he actively wrote about them in an essay that would become known as "A Report from Occupied Territory." This piece described what it was like to be an African American living in an environment that felt like a police state occupied by armed enforcers.

By the end of the decade, however, and on into the early 1970s, Baldwin's revolutionary fervor began to wane. He began to enter into what would be his quiet period, where he would consolidate his time and energy in and around his adopted home of France. In the following years, he would write several more major works, including *No Name in the Street*, *If Beale Street Could Talk*, and *Just Above My Head*.

The autobiographical narrative of *No Name in the Street* has some particularly poignant accounts of the quiet state of disillusion that Baldwin was entering into. At one point, Baldwin writes that he is an "aging, lonely, sexually dubious, politically outrageous, unspeakably erratic freak." Baldwin had accomplished much, but even so, he was continued to question his own trajectory in life.

Conclusion

During the 1980s, James Baldwin was more disillusioned with his American homeland than ever. The president who occupied the White House during much of this decade—Ronald Reagan—was in many ways the antithesis of what Baldwin espoused as the American ideal. Certainly, many Americans adore Reagan. The man is often credited with ending the Cold War, but Baldwin didn't take too kindly to Reagan's political posturing. He saw Reagan as an aggressive perpetuator of American imperialism cloaked with the kind of religious conservativism that Baldwin loathed.

At odds with the status quo, Baldwin once again found refuge in his own rich world of thought and speculation. He had by this point settled in Saint-Paul-de-Vence, a picturesque village in the south of France. His home was always open to receive visitors, and his old friend Beauford Delaney could often be found painting in the back garden. Baldwin continued working during these years, and his final book, *The Evidence of Things Not Seen*, was written in his house in Saint-Paul-de-Vence. He also became an important voice for the emerging gay rights movement, as he penned essay after essay on the themes of homosexuality and homophobia.

His musings would come to an end, however, on December 1, 1987, when he passed away from stomach cancer aged 63. On that day, James Baldwin left a world that he often found both infuriating and fascinating. He quietly passed on while simultaneously leaving behind a legacy that was louder than life.

Bibliography

Campbell, James (1991). *Talking at the Gates: A Life of James Baldwin.*

Craven, Alice Mikal & Dow, William E. & Nakamura, Yoko (2019). *Of Latitudes Unknown: James Baldwin's Radical Imagination.*

Farber, Jules B. (2016). *James Baldwin: Escape from America, Exile in Provence.*

Leeming, David (1994). *James Baldwin: A Biography.*

Mullen, Bill (2019). *James Baldwin: Living in Fire.*

Waters, Rob (2013). "Britain is no longer white": James Baldwin as a witness to postcolonial Britain. Accessed from http://sro.sussex.ac.uk/id/eprint/66547/

FBI Records of James Baldwin. Accessed from https://vault.fbi.gov/james-baldwin